SPACE STATIONS

ROBIN KERROD

WORLD ALMANAC® LIBRARY

Please visit our web site at:
www.worldalmanaclibrary.com
For a free color catalog describing
World Almanac® Library's list of high-quality
books and multimedia programs, call
1-800-848-2928 (USA) or **1-800-387-3178**
(Canada). World Almanac® Library's fax:
(414) 332-3567.

Library of Congress Cataloging-in-Publication Data

Kerrod, Robin.
    Space stations / by Robin Kerrod.
        p. cm. — (The history of space exploration)
    Includes bibliographical references and index.
    ISBN 0-8368-5710-0 (lib. bdg.)
    ISBN 0-8368-5717-8 (softcover)
    1. Space stations—Juvenile literature.   I. Title.
    II. Series.
    TL797.15.K47   2004
    629.44'2—dc22   2004049071

First published in 2005 by
World Almanac® Library
330 West Olive Street, Suite 100
Milwaukee, WI 53212 USA

Copyright © 2005 by World Almanac® Library.

Developed by White-Thomson Publishing Ltd.
Editor: Veronica Ross
Designer: Gary Frost, Leishman Design
Picture researcher: Elaine Fuoco-Lang

World Almanac® Library editor: Carol Ryback
World Almanac® Library designer: Kami Koenig
World Almanac® Library art direction: Tammy West

Photo credits: top (t), bottom (b), left (l), right (r)
All images used with the permission of NASA except:
Spacecharts Photo Library: 6, 8, 10 (artwork), 12, 18,
26, 27(b), 28, 29(t), 29(b), 30, 33(l), 33(r), 34(b), 41(b).
Novosti: 9, 11, 23(l), 24, 25. Artwork by Peter Bull.

Printed in Canada

1 2 3 4 5 6 7 8 9 09 08 07 06 05 04

Cover image: The International Space Station *in June 2002.*

Title page: Salyut 7 *in orbit.*

*Contents page: Cosmonaut Valery Polyakov gazes through
one of* Mir*'s windows.*

▼ *Space-walking astronauts on the* International
Space Station *in 2002.*

CONTENTS

HOMES IN SPACE

The biggest structure to ever orbit Earth, the *International Space Station (ISS)*, circles high above our heads. When completed, the *ISS* will stretch the length and nearly twice the width of a football field. It will be one-and-a-half times more massive than a Boeing 747 jumbo jet loaded with four hundred passengers. In fact, the *ISS* is so huge that it is easily visible to the naked eye and looks like a bright star moving slowly across the sky.

C rews from the United States, Russia, and other nations live and work on the *ISS* for months at a time. They perform experiments in physical sciences, biology, medicine, and engineering. These astronauts, scientists, and engineers are living the dreams of the pioneers of space travel, such as Russian Konstantin Tsiolkovsky, German Hermann Oberth, and American Robert Goddard. These men and others imagined people living and working in space stations in orbit around Earth. As the Space Age began in the 1950s, space scientists in the United States and the Soviet Union set their sights on space stations as a goal, too.

But when the thrust into space turned into a space race, both the United States and the Soviet Union put aside the idea of space stations and instead concentrated on landing men on the Moon. The United States succeeded, landing two *Apollo 11* astronauts on the Moon in July 1969.

Knowing it lost the Moon race, the Soviet Union switched its focus to the development of a space station. The result: The world's first space station, *Salyut* ("*Salute*"), which went into orbit in 1971. By then, the United States was getting ready to launch a space station of its own, named *Skylab* (for sky laboratory). It was launched in 1973.

▶ *A view of the* International Space Station *in December 2003 from the Space Shuttle Endeavour. The already impressive ISS grows in size as each new module is delivered and attached in orbit.*

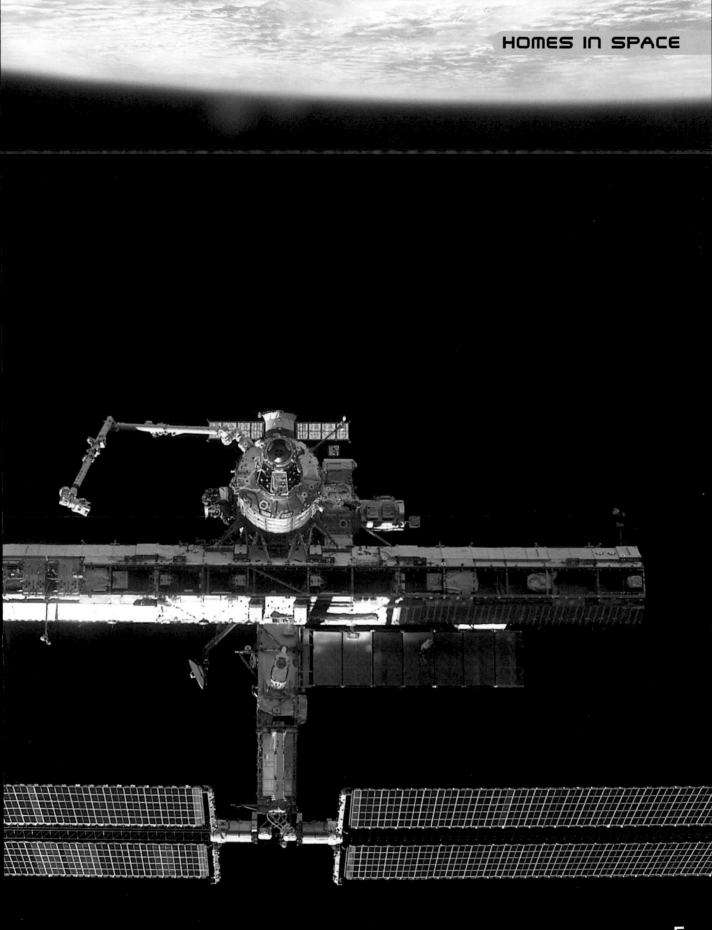

CHAPTER ONE

SALYUT AND SKYLAB

The first Soviet space station, *Salyut 1*, was not a great success, but it pointed the way ahead. The first U.S. space station, *Skylab*, was nearly crippled during launch, but then went on to be spectacularly successful.

In the late 1960s, the Soviet Union appeared to be keeping pace with the United States in a race for a lunar landing. By the end of 1968, it seemed ready to launch a cosmonaut in *Zond 7* on a journey around the Moon. He would be back even before three U.S. astronauts set off on a similar journey in *Apollo 8*. The Soviets expected a triumphant mission.

But the Soviet launch never occurred. Instead, a secret Soviet government meeting on January 1, 1969, determined that the main Soviet goal in space program would center around the launching of Earth-orbiting space stations. Soyuz spacecraft, originally developed for flights to the Moon, would ferry cosmonauts to and from their space station.

At the time—because of the extreme secrecy of the Soviet space program—observers in the West had no idea of this change in Soviet space goals. Most Westerners expected the Soviets to try to upstage the Americans, who were on the brink of a Moon landing.

A CHANGE OF PLAN

It became clear that the Soviet Union had changed the course of its space program after the joint flights of *Soyuz 4* and *5* in mid-January 1969. *Soyuz 4* took off on January 14 with a single cosmonaut on board;

▲ Soyuz 7 blasts off the launchpad at the Baikonur Cosmodrome in Kazakhstan on October 12, 1969. It rendezvoused in orbit with Soyuz 6 and Soyuz 8.

Soyuz 5 took off on January 15 with three cosmonauts on board. A day later, the two craft rendezvoused and docked to form a single unit. Two *Soyuz* cosmonauts donned space suits and floated through the hatch of the orbital compartment into space. Hand over hand, they inched their way to the open hatch of *Soyuz 4* and joined the cosmonaut there. After two orbits, the two craft separated and returned safely to Earth. Soviet newspaper *TASS* reported the "establishment of the first experimental orbital station"—which was, of course, yet another Soviet exaggeration and promotion of its space feats.

> " The time is not far off when a permanent space laboratory will be circling Earth. Scientists will go there for a tour of duty, working in comfortable surroundings and returning to Earth when necessary. "
> **Soviet academician Anatoli Blagonravov, speaking after the *Soyuz 4/Soyuz 5* linkup.**

A joint flight in October featured not two but three *Soyuz* craft—6, 7, and 8. They were launched a day apart and returned to Earth a day apart after nearly five days in orbit. An expected linkup between the three craft never materialized.

SPACE ENDURANCE

In a report on the October mission, *Soviet Weekly* wrote that, "The biggest problem involved in building orbital stations is the ability of man to remain long in space." This led to two cosmonauts in *Soyuz 9* lifting off in June 1970 for a long-term endurance flight.

The two cosmonauts—Andrian Nikolayev and Vitali Sevastyanov—stayed in space for more than seventeen days, nearly four days longer than the existing space endurance record set by the *Gemini 7*

STATION BENEFITS

Early manned spacecraft such as Vostok, Mercury, Gemini, and Apollo were small and lacked the facilities to support extended periods of time in space. We need space stations because they provide astronauts with relatively comfortable space homes in which people live and work for long periods. Space stations can also help us investigate the effects on the human body of long periods of weightlessness. Such studies are very important for further human exploration of space, including a return trip to the Moon, interplanetary flights to Mars, and voyages beyond. Space stations also provide unique conditions for the processing of materials. This could lead to the large-scale manufacturing in space of, for example, stronger alloys (mixtures of metals), more efficient computer chips, and purer drugs.

astronauts Frank Borman and James Lovell in 1965. The Soviets officially reported that their cosmonauts were in better health than expected after the flight. In fact, both men were very weak and could not walk for three days. It took them a month to recover.

FIRST SALUTE

Nevertheless, Soviet space scientists pushed ahead with plans for a space station in which cosmonauts could spend longer and longer times in space. The first hint that launch was imminent came in an interview with an unnamed Soviet "Chief Designer" in *Socialist Industry*, who said in March 1971 that it was "very expedient (useful) to build in the near future an orbital space station."

Westerners speculated that the Soviets would time their launch for April 12, the tenth anniversary of the first manned flight into space by Yuri Gagarin. Instead, the launch of the space station, *Salyut 1,*

▲ *A Soyuz spacecraft (left) inches its way to dock with* Salyut 1, *in this contemporary Soviet artist's impression.* Soyuz 10 *made the first docking with the space station in April 1971.*

occurred a week later, on April 19, 1971. *Salyut 1* measured about 47 feet (14.4 meters) long. It had three main cylindrical compartments, including the narrow the docking compartment, designed for docking with Soyuz spacecraft. It also had two work compartments, the largest of which measured about 14 feet (4.2 m) across.

Compared with previous spacecraft, *Salyut 1* was spacious. It contained a living area with table and chairs, a treadmill for exercise, and plenty of storage lockers. *Salyut 1* was also fitted with telescopes, cameras, and other scientific instruments. Twin solar panels provided electrical power.

THE FIRST MISSIONS

Four days after launch, a three-man crew set out in *Soyuz 10* and easily rendezvoused and docked with the Salyut.

But something must have gone wrong, because the crew never entered *Salyut 1* and undocked from it after only five hours or so. They made what seemed to be an emergency return to Earth, landing under the cover of darkness. The Soviets denied any problems. It is likely, however, that some fault with the station occurred. Whatever happened, it prompted the commander, Vladimir Shatalov, to abort the mission and return to Earth early.

Less than two months later, *Soyuz 11* sped into orbit, again carrying a crew of three—Georgi Dobrovolsky, Vladislav Volkov, and Viktor Patseyev. This time, everything went smoothly—the crew docked with *Salyut 1* and spent nearly twenty-four days in the space station, easily beating the space endurance record of the *Soyuz 9* cosmonauts. They undocked on June 29, 1971, fired *Soyuz 11*'s retrorockets, and prepared to return to Earth.

Their descent module landed automatically, as usual. Everything seemed normal. But when the crew of the recovery helicopter opened the module's hatch, they found all the crew members dead.

What had killed them? Was it the effect of prolonged weightlessness? Had their hearts been weakened and then stopped when gravity took hold again? Would weightlessness prove to be a barrier to long stays in space? There were all kinds of speculations about the cause of death.

▼ *The ill-fated crew of* Soyuz 11, *who died when returning to Earth in June 1971. They are, from left: Viktor Patseyev, Georgi Dobrovolsky, and Vladislav Volkov.*

> " We know that after this grievous loss, the difficult and dangerous struggle against nature will be continued with the same firmness and consistency. The Soviet people are used to struggle and do not retreat in the face of obstacles. "
>
> **Soviet Communist Party newspaper *Pravda*, after the death of the *Soyuz 11* cosmonauts.**

Accident investigators said that it had nothing to do with weightlessness; during reentry, a descent-module seal had failed, allowing oxygen to leak from the capsule. The cosmonauts, who were not wearing space suits, all died instantly.

Work started immediately to modify Soyuz to avoid a similar disaster. *Salyut 1* was de-orbited in October 1971. Mission controllers fired its retrorockets to slow it down so that it fell from orbit. It broke up as it reentered the atmosphere,

and the debris fell into the Pacific Ocean out of harm's way.

LABORATORY IN THE SKY

A year later, while the Soviet Union picked up the pieces of its space station program, the National Aeronautics and Space Administration (NASA) was on the verge of launching its own first space station, named *Skylab*.

As far back as 1959, NASA's Space Task Group at Langley Research Center in Hampton, Virginia, recommended that the United States develop Earth-orbiting space stations and fly manned missions to the Moon—in that order.

In 1960, NASA Administrator Keith Glennan named this advanced man-in-space program Apollo. After President Kennedy's stirring speech in May 1961 that urged the nation to land astronauts on the Moon, Apollo became specifically a Moon-

landing program that claimed priority. NASA put aside plans for a space station until after the Moon landings and the cancellation of Apollo program.

The agency decided to build the space station *Skylab* using hardware left over from the Apollo program. *Skylab* was designed around an empty rocket stage (unit) of a Saturn V launch vehicle. The rocket stage measured about 48 feet (14.7 m) long and formed the largest section of *Skylab*, called the orbital workshop (OWS). It provided the main living quarters for the crew and included an equipment storage space and an area for conducting experiments. *Skylab* astronauts would travel to the space station aboard an Apollo spacecraft that consisted of command (crew) and service (equipment) modules (CSM).

Two large panels of solar cells on the orbital workshop as well as a windmill-like set of panels generated electrical power for *Skylab*. Telescopes and

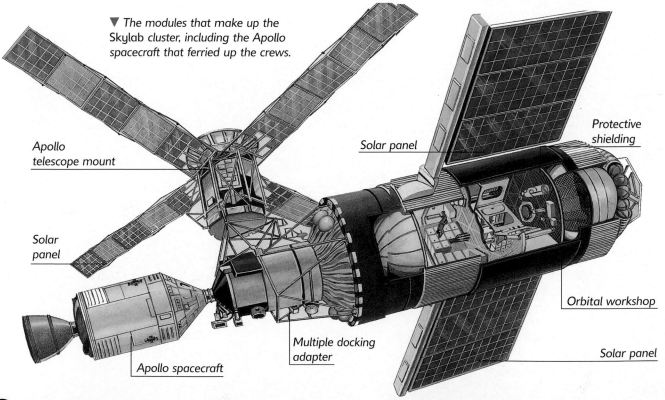

▼ The modules that make up the Skylab *cluster, including the Apollo spacecraft that ferried up the crews.*

Apollo telescope mount

Solar panel

Solar panel

Protective shielding

Orbital workshop

Multiple docking adapter

Apollo spacecraft

Solar panel

other instruments for studying the Sun were fastened to the "windmill." The entire unit was called the Apollo telescope mount.

When an Apollo spacecraft docked at one end, the *Skylab* cluster measured 119 feet (36 m) long. It had a mass of about 100 tons (90 tonnes) and would be the biggest structure ever to go into space. NASA planned to launch *Skylab* into orbit first, and three teams of three astronauts would then visit the station for increasingly longer periods.

INTO ORBIT

On May 14, 1973, a Saturn V launch vehicle carried *Skylab* into orbit. The first *Skylab* crew of three—Charles (Pete) Conrad, Joseph Kerwin, and Paul Weitz—were set to launch the next day.

Skylab thundered into an orbit about 270 miles (435 kilometers) high after what appeared to be a perfect launch (Mission *Skylab 1*). But it was not. Telemetry (signals) from *Skylab* showed that two

large solar panels on the OWS were not generating power. Sensors also indicated that shielding designed to protect the craft from meteorites and ultraviolet light was damaged. *Skylab* began to overheat in the unprotected solar radiation of space.

NASA delayed the first *Skylab* crew (Mission *Skylab 2*) flight while it figured out how to fix the underpowered and overheated space station. The mission eventually launched on May 25.

FIXING *SKYLAB*

In orbit, the *Skylab* astronauts discovered that one of the solar panels was missing and the other had jammed. A large section of the shielding had ripped off. Working through the open hatch of the air lock module, the crew erected a cover over the damaged section. The temperature inside *Skylab* soon began falling. A few days later, the crew also managed to unjam the remaining solar panel, finally giving *Skylab* enough power to function properly.

▲ Launch of Skylab by a Saturn V rocket. It marks the last launch of this gigantic rocket, originally designed to send astronauts to the Moon.

▲ The first crew to visit Skylab took this picture of the orbital workshop. It shows where Skylab's protective shielding had ripped away.

CHAPTER TWO

LIVING IN SKYLAB

The three teams of astronauts who visited *Skylab* smashed all space duration records. They proved that, in the right kind of spacecraft, humans can live and work in space for long periods.

Charles (Pete) Conrad, Joseph Kerwin, and Paul Weitz, the crew of the first manned *Skylab* mission, settled down to a heavy workload. They approved of their spacious quarters—*Skylab* had an internal volume of nearly 12,000 cubic feet (340 cubic meters), approximately the size of a semitrailer. It was nothing like the cramped capsules in which previous U.S. astronauts had traveled. The astronauts ate their meals at a table; they could shower; and they exercised on a bicycle. They could also exercise by running around the top section of the orbital workshop above the living quarters, using it like a race track.

They stayed in space for twenty-eight days, returning on June 22 and splashing down at sea in the Apollo command module. They broke the space endurance record in orbit set by the ill-fated *Soyuz 11* crew by four days. Conrad reported to the recovery crew: "Everybody here is in good shape." But were they? What had four weightless weeks done to their bodies? Physicians examined the astronauts carefully to find out. They found that each of them had a slightly weaker heart, muscles, and bones. But in general the men were remarkably fit, mainly because of the regular exercise sessions and running workouts they did while aboard *Skylab*.

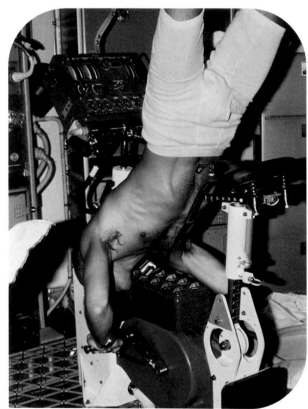

▲ *Pete Conrad chooses a novel way of exercising on* Skylab's *bicycle—pedaling with his hands!*

"It was a continuous and pleasant surprise how easy it was to live in zero gravity and how well you feel. ***Skylab* 2 astronaut Joseph Kerwin** I'd say very definitely that the average man or woman could fly in space. **Pete Conrad, one of the *Skylab* 2 astronauts, commenting on their mission.**"

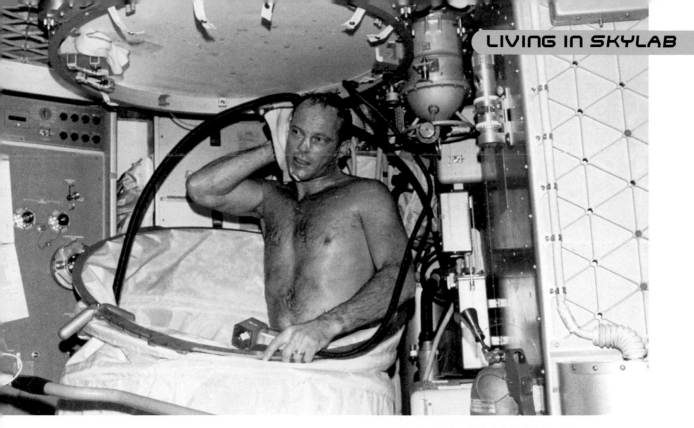

▲ Jack Lousma enjoys the luxury of a shower on Skylab. He squirts water onto his body from a showerhead and wipes himself with a cloth. Suction hoses remove any water droplets that might splash around.

SKYLAB 3

NASA decided to go ahead with the planned second manned mission (*Skylab 3*). But once again, the crew planned to make a few repairs. They had to put up another cover because the first was starting to break up. They would also have to replace some of the gyroscopes that kept *Skylab* in its proper attitude, or orientation, in orbit.

The new crew—Alan Bean, Owen Garriot, and Jack Lousma—flew up to *Skylab* on July 28, 1973. Unfortunately, they all began to suffer from space sickness, technically called space adaptation syndrome. Many astronauts experience this form of travel sickness. It causes feelings of nausea and sometimes even causes vomiting when the astronauts first experience weightlessness. Fortunately, as with most astronauts, the *Skylab* crew recovered quickly.

▲ A TV transmission from Skylab shows the astronauts eating a meal at the table in their living quarters.

BEATING RECORDS

The crew stayed in the space station for fifty-nine days, more than double the time of the previous crew. With its new cover and gyroscopes, *Skylab* remained in good shape. The only problem that developed concerned the Apollo CSM that had ferried up the crew. Fuel leaks in two of its four jet thruster units caused them to shut down. If another thruster unit failed, the crew might lose the ability to steer the Apollo spacecraft properly when they returned to Earth. NASA planned a rescue mission, but it proved unnecessary. The three men returned safely on September 25.

On November 16, Gerald Carr, Edward Gibson, and William Pogue traveled to *Skylab* on the final mission (*Skylab 4*). It ended eighty-four days later, on February 4, 1974. By then, *Skylab* astronauts had orbited Earth more than 1,400 times and traveled a total distance of more than 73 million miles (117 million km). It was a stunning space achievement.

THE *SKYLAB* EXPERIMENTS

On the three *Skylab* missions, the astronauts conducted more than 250 scientific investigations, many of which were specially designed to take advantage of the unique conditions of zero gravity in this great laboratory in the sky.

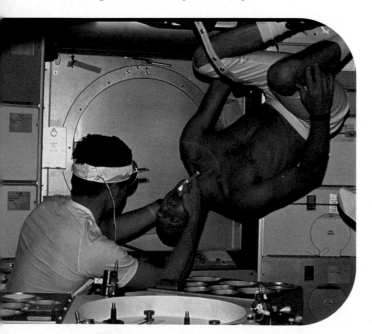

▲ Joseph Kerwin examines Pete Conrad's teeth on Skylab. In space, no dentist's chair is needed!

▼ Paul Weitz (top) fits a blood pressure cuff to Joseph Kerwin's arm. Weitz appears to be upside down in the photograph, but we can't really say he's upside down because there is no "up" or "down" in zero gravity.

One of the major study areas was space medicine—investigating how spaceflight affects humans. The astronauts took regular blood samples from one another and participated in experiments that monitored their heart and circulatory activity.

Under the weightless conditions, the astronauts grew taller by 1 inch (2.5 centimeters) or more. This happened because the vertebrae in the spine pulled apart slightly. The astronauts also appeared to slim down as fluids shifted upward from the lower parts of their bodies. These effects, and the weakness the astronauts experienced in their cardiac output, muscles, and bones, reversed themselves over time after the astronauts returned to Earth. Overall, the results of the experiments on human health were very encouraging.

> "From what we know today, there is no medical reason to bar a two-year mission to Mars.
> **Dr. Charles Berry, NASA director of Life Sciences, speaking after reviewing *Skylab* medical experiments.**"

SPACE SPIDERS

High school science students suggested some of the experiments carried out on *Skylab*. One study observed how spiders spun webs in weightless conditions (on *Skylab 2*). A spider named Arabella seemed disoriented at first, but then spun a normal web resembling those that it spun on Earth. Later on, its sister spider, named Anita, spun a normal web almost immediately. Researchers theorized that the second spider had had time to adapt to zero gravity.

▼ *Space spider Arabella spins its web.*

SPACE PROCESSING

The *Skylab* astronauts also did valuable work on processing materials in weightless conditions. They prepared crystals and produced new alloys (mixtures of metals) that tested out as being much stronger than similar materials prepared on Earth. Because of the lack of gravity, the particles in these materials mixed thoroughly, assuming their ideal

positions in their crystal structure. (Earth's gravity distorts and weakens these crystal structures.) The astronauts also found that they could weld metals easily using electron beams—something that could prove useful when building structures in space.

OBSERVING EARTH

The astronauts spent a lot of time observing Earth, using the instruments of the Earth-Resources Experiments Package (*EREP*). They took thousands of images of Earth in visible light and in other invisible wavelengths, such as infrared.

By studying these multiwavelength photographs, scientists found that they could identify a number of different surface features not ordinarily visible in regular photographs. This study proved how valuable remote-sensing satellites such as *Landsat* might be for mapping, land use and agriculture, pollution monitoring, and mineral prospecting.

▲ Skylab *picture of the Yazoo Basin on the lower Mississippi River.*

STUDYING THE SUN

Skylab's most spectacular results came from the study of the Sun. The astronauts spent hundreds of hours observing the Sun, using the instruments on the Apollo telescope mount. They took tens of thousands of photographs in many wavelengths, including X-ray, ultraviolet, and infrared.

By studying these different wavelengths of solar radiation, the *Skylab* astronauts could investigate all kinds of solar phenomena, such as solar flares and sunspots. Solar flares are enormous explosions on the Sun that shoot streams of high-energy particles into space. Sunspots are darker, cooler patches on the Sun associated with magnetic activity. In recent years probes such as *Ulysses* and *SOHO* greatly improved the amount and type of date gathered by these observations.

EXTRAVEHICULAR ACTIVITIES

The *Skylab* crews also performed their fair share of space walking, or EVAs (extravehicular activities). They spent a total of more than forty hours outside *Skylab* carrying out repairs and experiments.

SKYLAB'S FIERY FALL

Skylab orbited about 270 miles (435 km) from Earth. Even at that height, however, traces of the atmosphere produce drag that slows down and eventually drops a spacecraft from orbit. On July 11, 1979, *Skylab* broke up when it reentered the atmosphere, leaving a luminous trail like a gigantic meteor. Flaming *Skylab* debris rained down over a sparsely populated area in western Australia.

LOOPING THE LOOP

Prominences are perhaps the most spectacular solar events. These fountainlike eruptions of hot gas from the Sun can climb hundreds of thousands of miles into space. The *Skylab* crews observed many spectacular prominences. On December 19, 1973, the *Skylab 4* astronauts saw a prominence that, at its peak, created an arch that spanned 370,000 miles (600,000 km) across the Sun's surface. This type of prominence is called a loop prominence. It forms this characteristic shape as it follows the invisible structure of the Sun's magnetic field.

▼ *The spectacular solar prominence of December 19, 1973.*

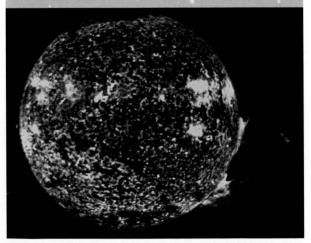

"*Skylab* has served us well as a true orbiting research facility, enabling our astronauts to carry out a wide spectrum of scientific, engineering, and biomedical studies. . . . *Skylab* has given us a wealth of new information about the dynamic processes of the Sun, provided new evidence of the value of Earth observations from space, helped define the feasibility of making new products in zero gravity, and has stimulated interest in international cooperation in space."
NASA administrator James Fletcher, February 1974.

▶ Skylab *viewed by the third and final crew of the space station as they left it in February 1974. The gold parasol, or sunshade, erected over the damaged section of Skylab's orbital workshop is clearly visible.*

CHAPTER THREE

COSMIC COOPERATION

Former space rivalries between the United States and the Soviet Union ended in 1975 when an Apollo spacecraft linked up with *Soyuz 19* in orbit. Still, the two countries did not conduct joint space operations for another twenty years.

By the time the last *Skylab* astronauts returned to Earth early in 1974, NASA was developing a totally new space transportation system—the Space Shuttle. Unlike the Apollo spacecraft that preceded it, each Shuttle was a reusable craft, designed for repeated journeys into space.

The Apollo program would officially end with a historic first American/Soviet linkup in space. The joint mission, called the *Apollo-Soyuz Test Project* (*ASTP*), began in 1972. President Richard M. Nixon approved the project as part of his policy of working to improve relations between East and West. Nixon and Soviet prime minister Alexei Kosygin agreed to the space plan on May 24, 1972. The mission was launched in July 1975.

Initially, planners hoped to launch Apollo and Soyuz to dock with a Salyut space station—forming an impressively large orbital complex, but the Soviets withdrew Salyut from the mission only a month later; only the Apollo and Soyuz spacecraft would dock.

▲ *Soyuz 19 lifts off the launchpad on July 15, 1975.*

THE CREWS AND THE CRAFT

Thomas Stafford, Donald Slayton, and Vance Brand were the American astronauts chosen for the historic flight. Veteran astronaut Stafford had flown two Gemini missions. He was also a crew member of the *Apollo 10* dress-rehearsal mission for the first lunar

landing. Slayton and Brand would both make their first flights on *ASTP*.

The Soviet crew member Alexei Leonov had flown previously in *Voskhod 2*, when he made the world's first space walk. Crewmate Valery Kubasov had flown a Soyuz mission once before.

The U.S. craft was an Apollo command and service module, like the one used to carry the *Skylab* astronauts, but with an important difference: It was attached to a docking module equipped for linking with the Soyuz spacecraft. The unit was also designed to act as an air lock, since the two spacecraft used different atmospheres. Apollo used pure oxygen at low pressure, while the Soyuz used a nitrogen/oxygen mixture at Earth's atmospheric pressure.

LIFTOFF

The mission finally began on July 15, 1975. The Soyuz (*Soyuz 19*) lifted off first from the Baikonur Cosmodrome in Kazakhstan that morning. The Apollo blasted off from the Kennedy Space Center in Florida that afternoon.

Over the next two days, the two craft maneuvered toward each other. Around midday, Florida time, on July 17, the two craft from the former bitter space-race rivals performed a perfect docking maneuver.

▼ *A NASA artist's impression shows the Apollo and Soyuz linkup in space via the docking module.*

▼ *An Apollo craft lifts off from the Kennedy Space Center.*

Leonov: "Capture!" **Stafford:** "We also have capture . . . we have succeeded. Everything is excellent." **Leonov:** "Soyuz and Apollo are shaking hands now." **Stafford:** "We agree."
Leonov: "Well done Tom. It was a good show. We're looking forward now to shaking hands with you on board Soyuz."
Conversation between Apollo commander Thomas Stafford, speaking Russian, and Soyuz commander Alexei Leonov, speaking English, during docking.

HANDSHAKE IN ORBIT

After Apollo and Soyuz docked, Stafford and Slayton transferred to the docking module, equalized the pressure to that in Soyuz, and opened the hatch to the Soviet spacecraft. Stafford floated through and shook hands with Leonov, symbolizing an unusual spirit of cooperation between the two great space powers. Over their two days together, the two crews visited each other's spacecraft, exchanged presents, ate meals together, and conducted a few joint experiments. They conducted live television transmissions from *Apollo-Soyuz*. Crew members also spoke with U.S. president Gerald Ford and Soviet premier Leonid Brezhnev.

The two craft separated on July 19, with Soyuz returning to Earth two days later. The usually secretive Soviets broadcast the landing live on TV stations around the world. Apollo continued to orbit for another three days, conducting a range of experiments and observations of stars and Earth.

▲ Apollo commander Donald Slayton floats through the hatch of the docking module to shake hands with Soviet commander Alexei Leonov.

▼ Cosmonauts Valery Kubasov (left) and Alexei Leonov work in the orbital module of the Soyuz spacecraft during the ASTP mission.

SPLASHDOWN

Apollo returned to Earth on July 24 in a nearly disastrous splashdown in the Pacific Ocean. Poisonous nitrogen dioxide fumes from the Apollo capsule's rocket thrusters leaked into the crew cabin. Stafford and Slayton managed to don their oxygen masks in time, but Brand did not and passed out for a short time. The three recovered when the opened hatch let in fresh air but they also spent several days in the hospital before NASA's doctors allowed their release.

APOLLO FINALE

The *ASTP* signaled the end of the seven-year Apollo era of space travel. During its reign, Apollo spacecraft carried thirty-six U.S. astronauts on twelve separate flights, including nine missions that orbited the Moon and six that landed. Apollo had one "successful failure"—*Apollo 13*—the mission that nearly cost the lives of its three-man crew.

Still, the Apollo story may continue. Ex-Apollo personnel have suggested that a larger, modified version of Apollo may someday carry crew members to the *International Space Station*.

> I am confident that the day is not far off when space missions made possible by this first joint effort will be more or less commonplace.
> **U.S. president Gerald Ford**
> It could be said that the *Soyuz-Apollo* is a prototype of future orbital stations.
> **Soviet premier Leonid Brezhnev**
> It was the world's most expensive handshake, but it will not have cost a dollar or ruble too much if it is a handclasp for peace.
> **London's *Sun* newspaper comments on the linkup, July 1975.**

▼ *Thomas Stafford (left) and Donald Slayton toast the Soviet crew with borsch (beet soup). They added humor to the occasion by pasting Vodka labels over their soup containers.*

CHAPTER FOUR

SALYUT SUCCESSES

The Soviet Union had little luck with its space station program until the launch of *Salyut 6*. Over its three-and-one-half-year lifetime, *Salyut 6* was manned almost continuously by teams of cosmonauts, who stayed in space for longer and longer periods.

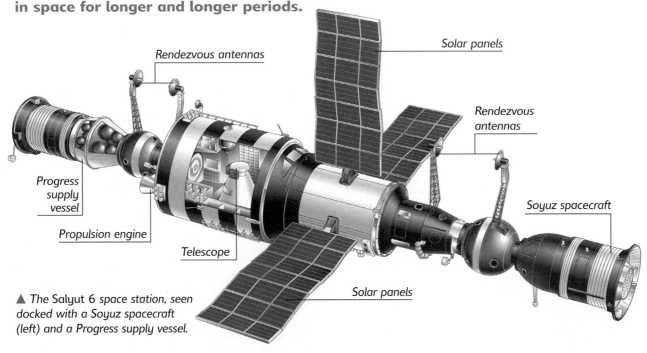

Rendezvous antennas

Solar panels

Rendezvous antennas

Progress supply vessel

Soyuz spacecraft

Propulsion engine

Telescope

Solar panels

▲ The Salyut 6 *space station, seen docked with a Soyuz spacecraft (left) and a Progress supply vessel.*

Despite the disastrous debut of *Salyut 1* in 1971 (*see* pages 8–9), the Soviet Union continued with its space station program. A second Salyut was launched in April 1972 but blew up after less than two weeks in orbit before any crew visited it. Lack of details about its design suggested that it was intended for military use. It also transmitted data at radio frequencies used by reconnaissance satellites. This action suggested that *Salyut 2* was very likely launched to test new photo reconnaissance (spy) equipment for taking high-

resolution photographs of the ground. Such images could pinpoint troop locations and movements.

SECRET LAUNCHES

More secrecy than usual also surrounded the launch of the next space station, *Salyut 3*, in June 1974, which was visited by the crew of *Soyuz 14* shortly afterward. The presence on board *Soyuz 14* of a military engineer and the use of military radio frequencies for communication also marked this as a military mission. The next crew (*Soyuz 15*) tried unsuccessfully to dock with the space station in August, and by December, as *Salyut 3* plunged back toward Earth, *Salyut 4* was launched.

Two crews (from *Soyuz 17* and *18*, respectively), occupied *Salyut 4*—first for one month and then for two months. *Soyuz 18* landed shortly after *Soyuz 19* touched down at the end of the *Apollo-Soyuz Test Project* mission (*see* Chapter 3). No other crews inhabited *Salyut 4*. Two crews also visited the next space station, *Salyut 5*—also intended mainly for military use. Launched in June 1976, it remained in orbit until August 1977.

SALYUT 6

A month after *Salyut 5* landed, the next Salyut space station headed for orbit. *Salyut 6* had the same basic shape as previous Salyuts—three cylinders of different diameters—but it was better equipped to support longer and more complex missions. *Salyut 6* had several powerful cameras for mapping the Earth and studying its resources, as well as telescopes for making astronomical observations. Its air locks exposed the onboard experiments to the space environment and allowed cosmonauts to perform EVAs, also called space walking missions.

Another major difference was that *Salyut 6* had two docking ports—one at each end. The reason for the second docking port became clear on the second manned mission to *Salyut 6* (*Soyuz 26*), launched in December 1977. The following month, an unmanned supply vehicle called *Progress 1* automatically docked at the second port. It carried rocket propellants, compressed air, food, water, parcels, films, and other scientific equipment.

Progress 1 was a stripped-down Soyuz craft, with no provision for landing. After its mission (and filled with waste), it was de-orbited and

▼ Columbia *lifts off the launchpad at the Kennedy Space Center on its fifth flight into space in November 1982.*

A NEW BIRD

Between the joint U.S./Soviet mission of July 1975 and early April 1981, the Soviet Union flew twenty-two manned missions. The United States flew none. Instead, it concentrated on launching the reusable but delayed Space Shuttle. Finally, on April 12, 1981, the Shuttle made its space debut, when *Columbia* flew into orbit. In November, *Columbia* climbed back into space on the first time return flight of any spacecraft.

▲ *Cosmonauts Viktor Savinykh (left) and Vladimir Kovalenok train in a mock-up of* Salyut 6 *in 1981.*

destroyed during reentry. With the use of Progress supply vessels, the Soviet Union had solved one of the problems of long-duration missions in space.

SALYUT 6 HIGHLIGHTS

The *Soyuz 26* cosmonauts remained in *Salyut 6* for more than ninety-six days, beating the space-endurance record set by the *Skylab 4* crew. Over the next three years, cosmonauts extended this record to more than 184 days.

▲ Salyut 7 *in orbit, with a Soyuz ferry docked at one end.*

Under a program called Intercosmos, *Salyut 6* was also visited by a succession of "guest cosmonauts" from other socialist countries, including Bulgaria, Cuba, Czechoslovakia, East Germany, and Vietnam. A Romanian guest flew on the last manned mission to *Salyut 6* in May 1981.

SALYUT 7

Salyut 6 eventually fell back to Earth in July 1982, but by then its successor had been in orbit for three months. The first crew to visit *Salyut 7* (*Soyuz T-5*) impressively beat the 184 days-in-space record set by *Salyut 6*, remaining in orbit for more than 211 days between May and December.

Crew members received a succession of visitors. Among the first three cosmonauts (on *Soyuz T-6*) was a French air force researcher named Loup Chrétien, the first Western European to fly in space. The second set of visitors (*Soyuz T-7*) included the second woman to ever fly in space.

THE FEMININE TOUCH

The Soviet Union had launched the first woman, Valentina Tereshkova, into space back in 1963. She flew primarily as a propaganda exercise to establish another Soviet space "first." In general, Soviet space scientists were not in favor of female cosmonauts. But they began to change their minds when, in 1978, NASA recruited its first female astronauts. The first U.S. female astronaut, Sally Ride, flew into space aboard Space Shuttle *Challenger* in 1983.

A Soviet mission designed to upstage Ride's flight occurred in August 1982, when *Soyuz T-7* carried Svetlana Savitskaya up to *Salyut 7*. Not just a "token female," Savitskaya began skydiving at sixteen, held world parachute records at seventeen, and at twenty-two became the world aerobatics champion. After an

▲ Svetlana Savitskaya and Vladimir Dzhanibekov talk with the Soviet media in July 1984, after their twelve-day mission to Salyut 7. They space walked for 3.5 hours.

aerobatics tournament in England, she was called "Miss Sensation."

Savitskaya returned to space in July 1984, when she performed the first space walk by a woman. This time she upstaged U.S. astronaut Kathryn Sullivan, who space walked three months later.

> "Cosmonautics is still in its infancy and life aboard spacecraft is extremely wearing, demanding, and physically difficult . . . including perhaps dangerous situations. . . . That being so, we feel the time is not yet right to impose such a strain on women.
> **Excerpt from an article in *Soviet Weekly*, March 1980.**

THINGS GO WRONG

While the *Soyuz T-9* crew was on board, things began to go wrong. In September 1983, fuel began leaking from *Salyut 7* and solar panels failed. The replacement crew scheduled to carry out repairs escaped with their lives when their launch vehicle exploded on the launchpad. Only the launch escape system saved their lives. This system consisted of a rocket unit that fired to lift the crew capsule clear of the rest of the launch vehicle.

The highlight of 1984 was the nearly 237-day flight of the *Soyuz T-10* crew. Only two missions arrived at *Salyut 7* in 1985, and the space station appeared to be failing. On the last mission, Soviet controllers suddenly recalled the cosmonauts "because of illness" when the young commander, Vladimir Vasyutin, suffered a nervous breakdown.

CHAPTER FIVE

MIR IN ORBIT

The launch of the Soviet spacecraft *Mir* introduced a new dimension into space station construction. *Mir* served as a core vehicle that could be expanded by adding on different modules.

Regular missions to *Salyut* 7 ceased in November 1985, following Vasyutin's illness. Three months later, a new Soviet space station joined it in orbit. Launched on February 20, 1986, the new station was named *Mir* ("Peace").

Not a complete space station, *Mir* was only the core module. It contained control equipment and living quarters, including individual cabins, a bathroom and washing area, and exercise equipment—complete with a treadmill. One end of *Mir* had a five-port docking unit. Its other end had yet another port.

Soyuz ferries and Progress supply craft would use these multiple ports to add on other experimental modules and resupply the craft.

TRICKY MANEUVERS

Leonid Kizim and Vladimir Solovyov, who currently held the space-duration record of nearly 237 days in space on board *Salyut* 7, flew up to *Mir* in March 1986. They checked out *Mir*'s systems. Two months later, they left *Mir* in their Soyuz—but not for Earth. Instead, they flew 2,000 miles (3,000 km) across

LIFE ON MIR

For the cosmonauts on board *Mir*, every minute was mapped out according to a strict timetable. Their days began at 8:00 A.M. Moscow time, when alarms on their watches went off. They divided their time between tending to the space station's equipment, conducting scientific experiments, eating their meals, and exercising by running on the treadmill and pedaling on the stationary bicycle. The cosmonauts prepared their own food using hot water to rehydrate packages of dehydrated foods. The standard menu included cabbage broth, beetroot soup, and porridge. In the evening, they would listen to favorite CDs or taped recordings of sounds of nature. The highlight of each week for the cosmonauts was a two-way video link with members of their families.

◀ Mir *in orbit in August 1987.*

space and docked with their old home, *Salyut 7*. The next month, they flew back to *Mir* for a few weeks before returning to Earth in July. By this time, Kizim had spent a total of more than a year in space.

In August, the *Salyut 7* craft was boosted to a higher orbit of about 300 miles (475 km) so that it was out of the operating orbit of *Mir*, which orbited at an altitude of about 200 miles (350 km).

GROUNDED

As missions to *Mir* enjoyed repeated successes from 1986 through 1988, the U.S. space effort struggled. Only three weeks before *Mir* launched, Space Shuttle *Challenger* exploded above Florida as it lifted off. The Shuttle fleet was grounded, and flights did not resume until September 1988.

▲ Floral tributes to Challenger's crew at their home base, the Johnson Space Center at Houston, Texas.

RECORD BREAKERS

As time went on, cosmonauts in *Mir* spent longer and longer times in orbit. In December 1988, two cosmonauts touched down after exactly a year in space. This record stood until March 1995, when Valery Polyakov returned after spending almost 438

▼ Valery Polyakov looks through one of Mir's windows during his record-breaking 437 days in orbit.

continuous days aboard *Mir*. His space-endurance record will stand for some time because the length of crew visits to the *International Space Station* averaged a few months (until the *Columbia* disaster).

THE *MIR* COMPLEX

The second crew to visit *Mir* did not take up residence until February 1987. They were on board when the first experiment module docked with the station the following month. *Kvant* ("*Quantum*") was a fully equipped science laboratory devoted mainly to astrophysics—the physics of the stars. It carried a series of astrophysical experiments, including X-ray and ultraviolet telescopes. The equipment had been developed with the European

Space Agency and individual European countries. Like the other modules to follow, *Kvant* was pressurized—filled with air under pressure—so that astronauts could work in it. *Kvant 2* was added to *Mir* in December 1989. As well as carrying scientific equipment, *Kvant 2* had a large air lock for cosmonauts to use when they went space walking.

KRISTALL, SPEKTR, AND PIRODA

The next module, *Kristall* ("*Crystal*") followed in June 1990, *Spektr* ("*Spectrum*") in June 1995, and *Piroda* ("*Nature*") in April 1996. The great gap in launch times between *Kristall* and the other two modules is linked to the timing of the Soviet Unions's breakup in December 1991.

Kristall, a technology module, contained furnaces for conducting experiments, such as melting metals to produce crystals of semiconductor materials for use in microchips. A docking module on *Kristall* allowed for future international visits from various spacecraft.

Spektr was a geophysical module, intended "for studies of the Earth's surface and atmosphere." It also served as a temporary home for U.S. astronauts when they stayed in *Mir*.

Piroda served as an international ecology research module. It used remote-sensing instruments that scanned Earth's surface at different wavelengths to study such things as the ocean-water surface temperatures, global wind speeds, and pollution.

MIR MISSIONS

During its incredible fifteen years in orbit, a total of 104 space travelers visited *Mir*. Of those, just forty-one were Russian cosmonauts. The others included forty-four Americans; six space travelers from France; four Germans; and one each from nine other countries, including Japan and Britain. French and German missions were financed by government space agencies or by ESA, the European Space Agency.

GOING COMMERCIAL

The Japanese mission to *Mir* was a commercial flight, financed by the Tokyo Broadcasting System (TBS) to

▲ European astronaut Ulf Merbold (center), pictured during his month-long stay in Mir in October 1994, with Alexsandr Viktorenko (left) and Yelena Kondakova (right).

celebrate its fortieth anniversary. In December 1990, despite suffering from space sickness, TBS journalist Toyohiro Akiyama spent six days aboard *Mir*, broadcasting live television and radio daily.

The British mission was financed by sponsorship. About 13,000 people answered an advertisement in the British press in July 1989: "Astronaut wanted. No experience necessary." Food technologist Helen Sharman was eventually selected and spent a week on *Mir* in May 1991.

MIR–SHUTTLE

The most significant "foreign" missions to *Mir*, however, were the visits by U.S. Space Shuttles.

▼ *Russian recovery personnel stand near a Soyuz descent module after it touched down in February 1996. It carried a cosmonaut crew returning from Mir.*

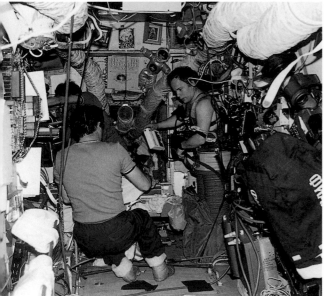

▲ *Yuri Gidzenko (foreground) and Sergei Avdeyev (right) at work in Mir in 1996. They conducted a joint mission with European astronaut Thomas Reiter (background).*

THE SOVIET UNION BREAKS UP

In December 1991, the Soviet Union disintegrated into fifteen separate republics. This followed negotiations within the Soviet Union under the direction of the president, Mikhail Gorbachev. The separate republics formed a new federation, known as the Commonwealth of Independent States. Each member had complete political independence. The Supreme Soviet of the USSR voted itself out of existence on December 26, 1991, bringing about the end of communist rule. (To reflect this change, we now use "Russian" rather than "Soviet" to refer to the former USSR space program because it is primarily a program of Russia.)

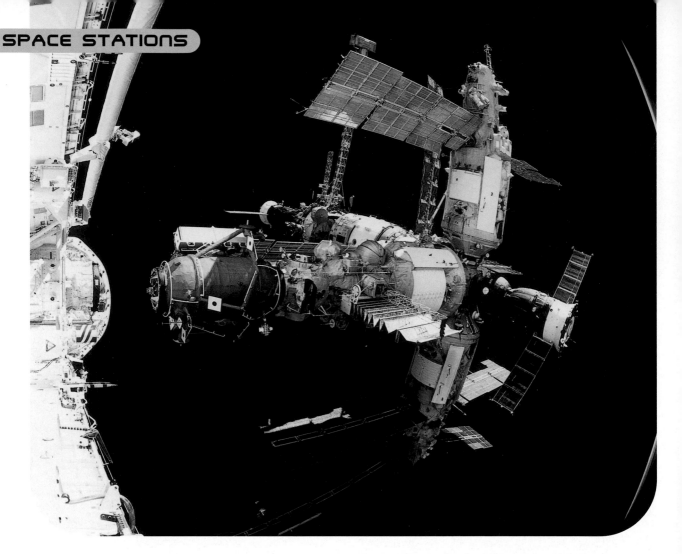

▲ *An IMAX camera in the payload bay of Space Shuttle* Atlantis *captured this stunning image of* Mir *with a fish-eye lens in November 1995 at the end of the second joint* Mir-Shuttle *mission.*

These flights were designed to provide U.S. astronauts and mission controllers experience in docking techniques in preparation for the construction of the upcoming *International Space Station* (*ISS*), and also in conducting joint operations with Russia, their main *ISS* partner.

The joint flights were preceded by the flight of a Russian cosmonaut (Sergei Krikalev) to the Space Shuttle *Discovery* in 1994, and a long-term stay on *Mir* by a U.S. astronaut (Norman Thagard, March-June 1995).

The first *Mir-Shuttle* flight in February 1995 saw the Space Shuttle *Discovery* rendezvous in orbit with *Mir* (Mission *STS-63*). Then in June, Space Shuttle *Atlantis* made the first docking with *Mir*. Eight further dockings followed through June 1998.

Over the three years of joint missions, one or another of the Shuttle spacecraft spent a combined total of forty-two days docked with *Mir*. Crews were exchanged, and U.S. astronauts spent a total of more than 900 days working in the space station. *Mir*'s two longest residents were American astronauts Shannon Lucid (188 days) and Michael Foale (145 days). Foale was on board during the emergency in 1997 when a Progress ferry collided with the *Spektr* module.

▲ Mir *and Space Shuttle* Atlantis *crews strike a pose. The first joint* Mir-Shuttle *mission in June 1995 achieved a number of milestones: It was the one-hundredth spaceflight by U.S. astronauts; it marked the first international space linkup since the Apollo-Soyuz Test Project in 1975; and it was the first time that ten astronauts gathered together in a single spacecraft.*

EMERGENCY!

The module *Spektr* served as living quarters for the U.S. astronauts who visited *Mir*. In June 1997, it was the temporary home of astronaut Mike Foale. But on June 25, an unmanned Progress supply vehicle crashed into *Spektr*. The collision damaged one of *Mir*'s solar panels and punctured its hull, causing it to depressurize, or lose its air. The crew quickly sealed off the *Spektr* module before the entire craft depressurized. If that had happened, all aboard might have died.

THE FINALE

The injection of NASA funds for the joint flights had provided a lifeline for *Mir*. When those flights ceased, the Russians soon ran out of money, and delayed performing much needed maintenance on *Mir*. Subsequently, there were only three more missions to the aging and rapidly deteriorating space station. The last, financed by a Western consortium called MirCorp, returned to Earth in June 2000.

By the fall of that year, *Mir* was descending lower and lower in orbit. With no funds available, *Mir* controllers decided to abandon the space station and made plans to bring it down from orbit. On March 23, 2001, *Mir* reentered the atmosphere, burning up as it plunged into the Pacific Ocean.

The death of *Mir* marked the end of a remarkable period of Russian space science. When *Mir* was launched in 1986, the Soviets believed that *Mir 2* would be in use by 1992. But funding dissolved, and *Mir 2* never materialized. Instead, the original *Mir* remained in orbit for another nine years, well past its expected usefulness. For ten years of its fifteen-year life span, *Mir* was permanently occupied. Even for its technically superior successor, the *International Space Station*, the trusty *Mir* will prove a hard act to follow.

> *Mir* has done an exceptionally fine job. Now it's time to give it a very respectful retirement.
> **Apollo 13 commander James Lovell, in June 1997, after the Progress collision with *Mir*.**

CHAPTER SIX

INTERNATIONAL SPACE STATION

When complete, the *International Space Station*—the largest and most complex project ever attempted in the history of spaceflight—will be four times the size of its famous predecessor, *Mir*.

NASA first discussed building a space station in 1969, but went on to develop the *Space Transportation System*, or *STS*, instead. In 1982, when the Space Shuttle was finally declared operational, NASA concentrated on working out requirements for a space station. In April 1983, NASA administrator James Beggs outlined a space station program to President Ronald Reagan, who gave it the go-ahead in his State of the Union speech nine months later. Congressional funding followed, and four years later,

◀ *Space Station* Freedom *by artist Alan Chinchar (1991).*

> "We can follow our dreams to distant stars, living and working in space for peaceful, economic, and scientific gain. Tonight I am directing NASA to develop a permanently manned space station, and to do it within a decade."
>
> **Extract from President Reagan's State of the Union address, January 25, 1984.**

in June 1988, President Reagan named the space station project *Freedom*.

By this time, the United States had acquired international partners in *Freedom*—Canada, the European Space Agency, and Japan. In 1991, the partners met with the Soviets to consider the possibility of using their Soyuz spacecraft as crew rescue vehicles. At the time, plans were underway for a replacing the aging *Mir* with a new station named *Mir 2*. (Again, that never happened.)

In 1993, President Bill Clinton ordered a redesign of *Freedom* to reduce costs. Discussions turned toward the idea of merging the *Freedom* and *Mir 2* programs. From a choice of two simplified space station plans, Clinton selected the one that combined *Freedom* and *Mir 2*: The *International Space Station* was born.

IMPRESSIVE

The *ISS* is an impressive structure. When completed, it will measure about 260 feet (80 m) long and 355 feet (108 m) across, with a mass of more than 1 million pounds (450 tonnes). The *ISS* orbits at an altitude of about 250 miles (400 km). (To imagine how far this is in a horizontal direction, consider that it matches the distance between Milwaukee, Wisconsin, and Detroit, Michigan.) At this altitude, the *ISS* orbits Earth at a speed of around 17,500 miles per hour (28,000 kph), circling our planet about every ninety minutes. *ISS* crew members see the Sun rise and set sixteen times daily.

NASA has played the biggest role in designing and building the *ISS*, which is being assembled piece by piece in orbit from modules ferried up to it. Two major launch vehicles are involved—Russia's powerful Proton rocket and, until early 2003, the U.S. Space Shuttle fleet. It may take as many as forty-five flights to assemble the entire station.

Modules join together through a combination of automatic docking, robotic devices, and hands-on manipulations and connections by space-walking astronauts. It may take up to 160 EVAs before the *ISS* is complete—which will probably not happen before 2008.

▲ ISS nodes (see page 34) under construction at the Marshall Space Flight Center in Huntsville, Alabama.

▲ *Work in Russia on the functional cargo block (FCB) for the ISS, later named Zarya and launched in 1998.*

THE *SPACELAB* EXPERIENCE

Scientific work on the *ISS* is carried out in a number of laboratory modules. To a large extent, these evolved from a space laboratory called *Spacelab*, flown on the Space Shuttle between 1983 and 1995. *Spacelab*, built by the European Space Agency, was a cylindrical unit about 23 feet (7 m) long and 13 feet (4 m) in diameter that contained a fully equipped laboratory. Experimental instruments lined its walls. A window allowed astronauts to observe Earth.

UP AND AWAY

The first *ISS* assembly flight lifted off November 20, 1998, when a Proton rocket carried a module called *Zarya* ("*Sunrise*") into orbit. Although the Russians built *Zarya*, the U.S. designed and financed it.

Space Shuttle *Endeavour* delivered the first U.S. module—a structure called a node—to the *ISS* in early December. Named *Unity*, it is fitted with six berthing ports which allow other units to connect with it. Two more Space Shuttle flights in May and December 1999 carried supplies to *Zarya* ahead of the arrival of the first crew to occupy the station.

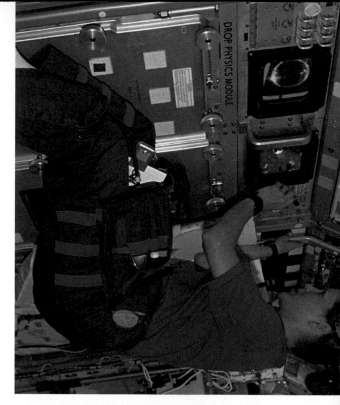

▲ *Kathryn Thornton works inside Spacelab on Space Shuttle Mission STS-73 in October 1995. She and six other astronauts spent nearly sixteen days conducting experiments in crystal growth, fluid dynamics, and biology.*

▼ *Cutaway artwork shows how Spacelab fits inside the Space Shuttle's payload bay. Scientist-astronauts work in Spacelab's cylindrical module.*

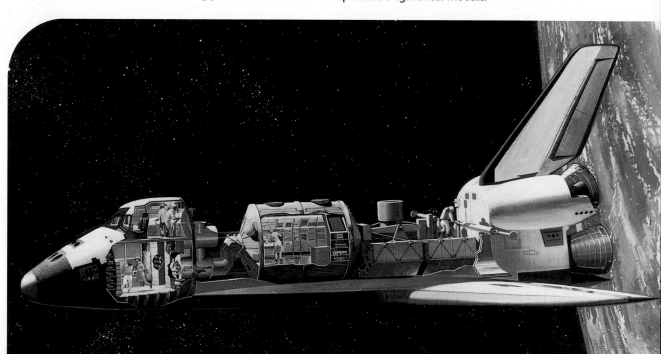

Manned crews only became possible after the much-delayed, Russian-built service module, called *Zvezda* ("*Star*"), was attached to *Zarya* in July 2000. The first crew took up residence that October.

Further Shuttle missions in 2000 ferried up solar panels mounted on truss structures (crisscrossed metal frameworks) to give the *ISS* extra power. (Both *Zarya* and *Zvezda* had their own solar panels.) The extra power was needed when the U.S. laboratory module *Destiny* linked with the *ISS* in February 2001. Another important launch in 2001 included the attachment of Canada's robot arm (*Canadarm 2*) to assist in further assembly work.

More truss structures followed in 2002, as crews shuttled back and forth, spending between four and

CANADA'S CANADARM

The main robot arm installed to assist in the assembly of the *ISS* has been provided by Canada. It is based on the *Canadarm*, the robot or RMS (remote manipulator system) arm fitted in the payload bay of the Space Shuttle. It is basically a very versatile crane. It can pick up objects from the Shuttle's payload bay and place them in position on the *ISS*. Later, it will be used to handle equipment for maintenance work on the *ISS*. The *Canadarm* is nearly 60 feet (16 m) long and has flexible joints and a metal fixture for gripping. It has a wide range of uses because it is mounted on a mobile platform that can travel along the main truss of the *International Space Station*.

six months in orbit at a time. Expedition crews either traveled to the *ISS* aboard Russia's Soyuz spacecraft or via one of the U.S. Space Shuttles. Visitors returned to their respective home countries on whichever space vehicle was available.

▲ Space Shuttle Endeavour, *carrying the* Unity node (in the foreground), *closes in on* Zarya *in December 1998.*

▼ James Newman *lends a hand to help link* Unity *with* Zarya. *Space Shuttle* Endeavour *is reflected in his visor.*

▲ Inside the U.S. laboratory module Destiny in February 2001. The first Expedition crew members pose in the foreground. Behind them stand the visiting crew members of Space Shuttle Atlantis.

DESTINY

The U.S. laboratory module, *Destiny,* is the focus of scientific research on board the *ISS*. Made up of three cylindrical sections, *Destiny* measures about 29 feet (8.8 m) long and 14 feet (4.4 m) across. Like *Spacelab*, it is fitted with more than twenty experimental racks. It also has a window to allow Earth observations.

Destiny also functions as the command and control center for the entire *ISS* complex. It is where the main environmental and life-support systems that provide the station with a pressurized, comfortable atmosphere are located. *Destiny* is linked to the multiple berthing node *Unity*; so is another U.S. module called the *Quest* joint air lock. This unit provides access into space for space walking

astronauts. Also, the U.S and Russian space suits are stored in *Quest*.

Original *ISS* plans called for the U.S. to supply a habitation module. It would have provided extra living accommodations, including a toilet, shower, sleep stations, and medical facilities to serve a bigger space-station crew, but it was eliminated from the budget. It is possible that the Italian Space Agency module may now build that module in time for launching in 2007 or 2008.

The truss sections that the United States supplies form the "backbone" of the *ISS*. These trusses support the main solar panels that capture solar energy and convert it into the electricity that powers the *ISS*.

THE RUSSIAN MODULES

The first task of the Russian module *Zarya*, the first section of the *ISS* that was launched, was to provide early power, propulsion (forward thrust), steering, and communications for the new station. Now it is used as a passageway, docking port, fuel tank, and storage facility. *Zarya* evolved from a redesign of a transport supply ship that flew to *Salyut* 6 and 7.

The Russian service module, *Zvezda,* provided the main living quarters for the crews in the first years. Originally designed for use in the *Mir 2* space station, which never flew, *Zvezda* consists of two cylinders of different sizes. The larger-diameter section accommodates the crew by providing sleeping quarters, cooking equipment, tables, exercise equipment, and bathroom facilities. At present, *Zvezda* is linked with a docking module called *Pirs* ("*Pier*"). This not only contains docking ports for use by Soyuz and Progress ferries but also provides an air lock for space walks.

Plans to extend the Russian segment of the *ISS* originally included two research modules. Future Russian participation is uncertain because funds for its space program are very limited.

> One can't fly to space without money. Sorry to say, but I believe that our space program is dying. **Veteran cosmonaut Georgi Grechko, quoted in the *Houston Chronicle*, October 2002.**

THE EUROPEAN MODULE

The main European *ISS* contribution is the *Columbus* laboratory module, provided by the European Space Agency. Officially called the *Columbus Orbital Facility*

▼ NASA artist's impression of the ISS when it is completed. The main laboratory and habitation modules are in the center. Long truss sections make up the station's framework and hold the solar cells that generate electrical power for the complex.

(*COF*), it has the same dimensions as the *Spacelab* that the ESA built for use on the Space Shuttle (*see* page 34). A range of experiments are planned for *Columbus*. They are centered around ten standard payload (cargo) racks, each of which is a miniature science laboratory. A materials-science laboratory investigates how crystals form in zero gravity. A fluid-science laboratory examines how liquids behave ("fluid dynamics"). A bio-lab conducts experiments on plants, animals, and microorganisms. A physiology lab studies how the human body responds to space by measuring physiological effects, such as muscle wasting and bone loss, heart rates, and blood-flow changes. Other experiments are mounted outside the module and exposed directly to outer space.

Another important ESA contribution to the *ISS* is the provision of a supply craft called an ATV, or Automated Transfer Vehicle. Launched by an Ariane 5

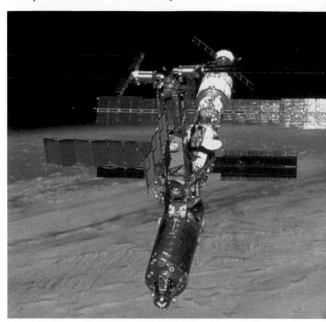

▼ *A beautiful view of the* ISS *taken from the Space Shuttle* Endeavour *in June 2002.*

▼ *Space-walking astronauts John Herrington (left) and Michael Lopez-Alegria work on one of the truss assemblies on the ISS in November 2002.*

rocket, the supply craft carry food, water, compressed air, electronic equipment, rocket propellants, and other essential items. The ATV will rendezvous and dock automatically with the *ISS*.

JAPAN'S *JEM*

Japan is also providing a laboratory module called *JEM* (*Japanese Experiment Module*), or *Kibo* ("*Hope*"). Like *Columbus*, it has an external facility for exposing payloads to open space. It is also fitted with a robot arm for handling these payloads.

AFTER *COLUMBIA*

The space station program faltered in February 2003, when Space Shuttle *Columbia* disintegrated when it reentered the atmosphere. NASA grounded the entire Space Shuttle Fleet, with further Shuttle missions not expected until 2005.

The task of changing Expedition crews and resupplying the station fell to the Russians and their manned Soyuz and unmanned Progress craft. In late April 2003, *Soyuz TMA-2* ferried the two-member *Expedition 7* crew up to the *ISS*. They were considered a "caretaker crew," sent to monitor the *ISS*, keeping it habitable and productive until full operations resume again with the Shuttle flights.

Early in May, the three *Expedition 6* astronauts experienced a particularly harrowing return to Earth in *Soyuz TMA-1* (*see box*). Fears about a basic problem with the Soyuz craft proved groundless after *Soyuz TMA-2*'s perfect descent in October 2003. It brought back the returning *Expedition 7* crew members after their stay aboard the *ISS*.

▶ *A Soyuz ferry craft edges in to dock with the International Space Station.* After Columbia *was lost and the Space Shuttle Fleet grounded, Soyuz provided the only way of transporting crews to and from the* ISS.

DANGEROUS DESCENT

On the evening of May 3, 2003, *ISS* Expedition 6 crew members Ken Bowersox and Don Pettit (both from the U.S.) and Nikolai Budarin (Russian) climbed into the *Soyuz TMA-1* spacecraft and prepared for their return to Earth. The Soyuz craft separated from the *ISS*, fired its retrorockets, and started to fall back to Earth. As the craft descended, the crew began experiencing G-forces of up to nine times the normal force of Earth's gravity. Something had gone wrong: The craft followed a much steeper trajectory than planned. This brought it down nearly 325 miles (500 km) from the expected landing site. Because of damaged radio antennae. Bowersox, Pettit, and Budarin couldn't communicate with anyone. Helicopter recovery crews searched for two hours before finding the men. Early suggestions that one of the U.S. astronauts caused the abnormal descent by "pushing the wrong button" were soon dismissed; a glitch in the spacecraft's computer caused the nearly fatal landing problem.

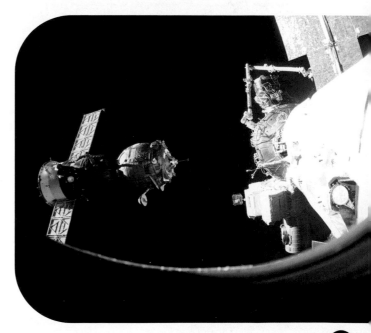

CHAPTER SEVEN

TO THE MOON AND MARS

In the future, a space station may serve in an expanded role as a spaceport for building and operating interplanetary spacecraft for bases on the Moon, Mars, and beyond.

Solar satellite power stations are among the structures that may someday be constructed in orbit. The Sun always shines in space. A space power station could capture and transform solar energy using huge panels of solar cells, solar reflectors, or some future solar technology not yet developed. The energy produced could then be beamed back to Earth or up to a space base.

▲ *Solar-power space stations may someday concentrate the Sun's energy and beam it to Earth or to a space base.*

MOON BASE

Astronauts last set foot on the Moon in 1972, but they will almost certainly return at some point in the future—most likely to set up a base on the lunar surface. A space station between Earth and the Moon would serve as a convenient site for assembling the hardware needed for repeated trips to a Moon base.

Astronauts setting up the first lunar base might possibly live on a space station and commute to the Moon on a regular basis or use it as an "oasis" in space for rest and relaxation.

The first Moon base will rely heavily on Earth for essential supplies, but someday lunar workers may grow their own food in greenhouse modules built partially on a space station. As Earth-based scientists continue to devise new technologies for space travel and habitation, people living in space may one day produce all the food, oxygen, water, and fuel they need with only occasional help from space stations. Complete recycling—reusing all resources—would no doubt become mandatory on all space stations.

PUSHING BACK THE FRONTIER

Even before a permanent Moon base is established, space explorers must plot their next logical step in the space frontier. Some might say that Venus is the obvious target. After all, Earth's nearest Solar System neighbor shares some of Earth's characteristics: It is considered a terrestrial planet, it has an atmosphere, and it is nearly the same size as Earth. The problems

Apollo 17 *astronaut Harrison Schmitt and the Lunar Rover at Taurus-Littrow during the last Moon landing.*

with Venus include its ovenlike temperatures (about 900° Fahrenheit or 480° Celsius), its body-crushing high atmospheric pressures, and a "weather system" of sulfuric acid clouds. Even if we established a space station between Earth and Venus, these many negative factors help rule out the human settlement of the second planet in our Solar System.

MISSIONS TO MARS

Mars, our next nearest neighbor in the opposite direction, seems much more suitable for humans. Although Mars is generally much colder than Earth, summer temperatures around its equator rise to

▼ *A NASA artist's impression of a materials processing facility at an early Moon base.*

THE NEW VISION

In a speech in January 2004, President George W. Bush called on NASA to "gain a new foothold on the Moon and to prepare for new journeys to worlds beyond our own."

" . . . We do not know where this journey will end, yet we know this: Human beings are headed into the cosmos. . . ."

First, the United States must complete the *International Space Station.* Second, the U.S. should begin developing a new manned exploration vehicle that can explore beyond Earth orbit.

"Our third goal," said Bush, "is to return to the Moon by 2020 as the launching point for missions beyond. . . . With the experience and knowledge gained on the Moon, we will then be ready to take the next steps of space exploration: human missions to Mars . . . ."

In closing, the president said: "We choose to explore space because doing so improves our lives and lifts our national spirit. So let us continue the journey."

above freezing. Mars' extremely low-pressure atmosphere contains some of the same elements that are found on Earth. Still, humans could not breathe martian air because it is 90 percent carbon dioxide with only small amounts of oxygen.

The biggest drawback about visiting Mars is distance. The Red Planet never comes closer to us than about 36 million miles (58 million km), and it is much farther away most of the time.

Using present technology, a crewed expedition to Mars and back would take between two and three years. Meanwhile, space scientists and

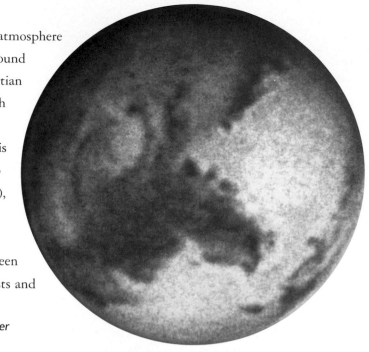

▶ Mars, the fourth planet from the Sun, comes closer to Earth than any other planet except Venus.

▼ In this artist's impression, astronauts emerge from a landing vehicle to begin exploring the surface of Mars, the "Red Planet."

engineers must solve many problems before such a mission can occur.

A MARS EXPRESS

We already have the technology to keep people alive in space for many months at a time. Space explorers owe much to the brave men and women who lived aboard the *Mir* Space Station during its many years of continuous operation. Likewise, Mars-bound astronauts, cosmonauts, and space travelers from other countries would all benefit from spending time on the *ISS* or some other future space station before leaving someday for the Red Planet.

Any logical plan to establish a "Mars Express" might very likely involve construction of one or two space stations between Earth and a base on Mars. (Future generations may someday marvel at space stations—much as we regard ancient sailing ships.)

SPACE-STATION REST STOPS?

In the distant future, interplanetary space stations could serve as rest areas, supply centers, repair shops, and first-aid stations for space travelers. They could also become research bases for studying the Universe free from atmospheric interference. While space stations would require special protection from the intense radiation of space, the development of the necessary technology for permanent space stations would also improve our lives on Earth in ways we can only imagine.

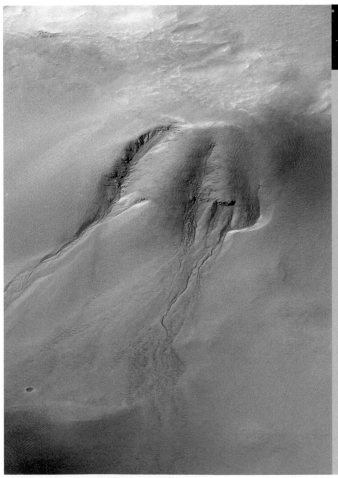

WATER, WATER EVERYWHERE

Centuries ago, astronomers spotted white caps at the north and south poles of Mars. They called these areas ice caps—even before understanding exactly what covered these polar regions. Space probes provided a closer look, and helped us determine that the polar caps consist of water ice as well as dry ice (frozen carbon dioxide). Probes also confirmed that water ice exists in the permanently frozen soil over much of the planet.

U.S. probes *Clementine* (launched 1994) and *Lunar Prospector* (1998) found evidence of water ice in some deep craters near the Moon's poles where solar rays never reach. Asteroids, comets, and meteoroids that bombarded the lunar surface may have carried water particles as well.

◀ *What seem to be water channels have eroded the walls of a meteorite crater on Mars in this image sent back by the* Mars Global Surveyor *probe.*

1957
October 4: The Space Age begins when the Soviet Union launches *Sputnik*.

1959
NASA suggests that the United States should consider building an Earth-orbiting space station.

1961
April 12: Soviet cosmonaut Yuri Gagarin in *Vostok 1* becomes the first human to orbit Earth.

1962
February 20: John Glenn becomes the first American in orbit, circling the Earth three times in *Friendship 7*.

1969
January: The Soviet government decides to concentrate on developing space stations.

July: NASA begins to plan a space station called *Skylab*.

1971
April 19: The first Soviet space station, *Salyut 1*, is launched. *Soyuz 11* cosmonauts stay in the Salyut for nearly 24 days, but are killed during reentry on June 29.

1972
January: President Richard M. Nixon approves plans for a reusable Space Shuttle.

April: *Salyut 2* launched, but explodes two weeks later.

May: President Nixon and Soviet prime minister Alexei Kosygin agree to a joint space flight, the *Apollo-Soyuz Test Project (ASTP)*.

1973
May 14: *Skylab* Space Station is damaged during launch.

May 25: The *Skylab 2* astronauts repair *Skylab*,

and its crew spends 28 days in orbit. The *Skylab 3* crew travels to *Skylab* for a 59-day stay, returning on September 25.

November 16: The *Skylab 4* crew flies up to *Skylab*.

1974
February 4: The *Skylab 4* crew returns from *Skylab* after a record 84 days in space. *Salyut 3* is launched in June; *Salyut 4* in December.

1975
July: The *ASTP* mission; Apollo and Soyuz spacecraft dock for two days.

1976
June: *Salyut 5* launched.

1977
September: *Salyut 6* launched.

1978
January: An automatic supply vessel, *Progress 1*, launched to *Salyut 6*.

1981
April 12: Space Shuttle *Columbia* ushers in the Space Shuttle era with a 54-hour round-trip into space. It returns to space in November.

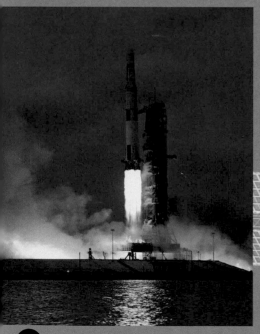

1982

April: *Salyut* 7 enters orbit. *Soyuz T-5* crew launches in May and extends space duration record to 211 days.

August: Soviet cosmonaut Svetlana Savitskaya visits *Salyut* 7 to become the second woman to fly in space.

1983

June: Sally Ride becomes the first American woman to fly in space in Space Shuttle *Challenger*.

December: The European-built *Spacelab* makes its debut on Shuttle Mission *STS-9*.

1984

January: President Ronald Reagan announces his approval for a U.S. space station, later named *Freedom*.

1986

January: *Challenger* explodes shortly after liftoff on Mission *STS-51L*, killing its crew of seven. NASA suspends all Shuttle flights.
February: Soviet Space Station, *Mir*, is launched.

1988

September: Shuttle flights resume with the launch of *Discovery* (*STS-26*).

November: The Soviet Space Shuttle *Buran* blasts off from the Baikonur Space Center.

1995

February: *Discovery* (*STS-63*) performs a rendezvous with the *Mir Space Station*.

March: Valery Polyakov returns to Earth after a record 437-day stay on *Mir*.

1996

March: Shannon Lucid flies in *Atlantis* (*STS-76*) to *Mir* for an extended mission. She returns in *Atlantis* (*STS-79*) in September after 188 days on *Mir*—the longest stay in space to date by any U.S. astronaut.

1998

November: Construction of the *International Space Station* (*ISS*) begins.

2000

October: A Soyuz spacecraft ferries the Expedition 1 crew members to take up residence in the *ISS*.

2001

March: *Discovery* carries up Expedition 2 crew and returns with the Expedition 1 crew.

2003

February 1: *Columbia* breaks up in the atmosphere when returning to Earth after a 16-day mission (*STS-107*). The crew of seven is lost; all Shuttle flights are suspended.

2005

Return to flight by the Shuttle Fleet projected for spring.

2008

Earliest possible date for completing construction of the *ISS*.

attitude
The way a spacecraft is orientated or positioned in space.

capsule
The name given to the tiny crew cabin of early manned spacecraft.

cosmonaut
The Russian name for a space traveler.

docking
The joining up of two spacecraft in space.

ESA
The European Space Agency, the organization that coordinates space activities in Europe.

EVA (ExtraVehicular Activity)
Time spent outside a spacecraft while in space; also known as space walking.

G-forces
The forces astronauts experience when their launch vehicle accelerates quickly beneath them.

launch vehicle
A combination of rockets used to launch spacecraft into orbit.

life support
A system in a spacecraft or space base that provides the necessary conditions to support human life.

mission control
The center that controls the flight of a spacecraft and crew activities in space.

module
A self-contained unit with a distinct function.

orbit
The usually circular or elliptical path in space taken by an object around a celestial body.

orbiter
The portion of the Space Shuttle that carries the crew and payload.

payload
The cargo a spacecraft carries.

probe
An unmanned spacecraft sent to explore celestial bodies, such as planets, asteroids, or comets.

reentry
The period during which a spacecraft returns to Earth's atmosphere.

rendezvous
The meeting of two spacecraft in space.

retrorocket
A rocket fired to slow down a spacecraft. A spacecraft fires its retrorockets as a brake to reduce its speed so that it can fall down from orbit.

rocket
A self-contained engine that burns fuel in oxygen to produce a stream of hot gases. As the gases shoot out backward through a nozzle, the rocket is propelled forward. Because they carry their own oxygen supply, rockets can work in space.

solar panel
A device that produces electricity by harnessing the energy in sunlight.

space medicine
Study of the effects of spaceflight on the body.

space sickness
Properly called space adaptation syndrome; an unpleasant condition experienced by many astronauts in the first few days of a mission.

stage
A rocket unit in a launch vehicle.

terraforming
Turning another planet into a replica of Earth.

thrusters
Smaller rockets on a spacecraft fired to help maneuver the craft in space.

truss
A crisscrossed metal structure designed to support loads, such as the solar panels of the *ISS*.

weightlessness
The strange state astronauts experience in orbit, when their bodies—and everything else—appear to have no weight at all.

BOOKS TO READ

Bond, Peter. **The Continuing Story of the International Space Station**. Springer-Praxis, 2003.

Burrough, Brian. **Dragonfly: NASA and the Crisis Aboard Mir**. HarperCollins, 2000.

Feldman, Heather. **Skylab: The First American Space Station**. Rosen Publishing, 2003.

Foale, Colin. **Waystations to the Stars: The Story of Mir, Michael, and Me**. Trafalgar Square, 1999.

Hall, Rex. **Soyuz** Springer-Verlag, 2003.

Launius, Roger. **Space Stations: Base Camps to the Stars**. Smithsonian Institution Press, 2003.

Linenger, Jerry. **Off the Planet: Surviving Five Perilous Months Aboard the Space Station Mir**. McGraw-Hill, 2000.

Pascoe, Elaine. **The International Space Station**. Gale Group, 2003.

Shayler, David. **Skylab: America's Space Station**. Springer-Verlag, 2001.

SPACE CAMPS

Florida, Alabama, and other locations host a number of space camps in the summer months. Lessons include learning about the nature and problems of spaceflight as well as "hands-on" experience in spaceflight simulators.
www.spacecamp.com
www.vaspaceflightacademy.org

PLACES TO VISIT

The shuttle fleet takes off from the Kennedy Space Center on Merritt Island, just inland from Cape Canaveral.

Guided bus tours of the launch facilities at the Kennedy Space Center and the Cape Canaveral Air Force Station occur daily. For details of upcoming events, check out the following web sites: www.nasa.gov/; www.ksc.nasa.gov/; and www.pao.ksc.nasa.gov/kscpao/schedule/schedule.htm.

The Johnson Space Center in Houston, Texas, has a visitors' center and rocket park. It is also home base for U.S. astronauts. For further details, see www.jsc.nasa.gov/ and http://spacecenter.org/.

Other air and space museums around the United States include:

International Women's Air and Space Museum, Cleveland, OH www.iwasm.org/

Intrepid Sea-Air-Space Museum, New York City www.intrepidmuseum.org/

Neil Armstrong Air and Space Museum, Wapakoneta, OH www.ohiohistory.org/places/armstron/

Oregon Air and Space Museum, Eugene, OR www.oasm.org/

Pima Air and Space Museum, Tucson, AZ www.pimaair.org/

San Diego Aerospace Museum, San Diego, CA www.aerospacemuseum.org/

The Smithsonian National Air and Space Museum (**NASM**), Washington, D.C. Exhibits include rockets and spacecraft such as Mercury, Gemini, and Apollo. www.nasm.edu/

U.S. Space and Rocket Center, Huntsville, AL www.ussrc.com

Virginia Air and Space Center, Hampton, VA www.vasc.org/

WEB SITES

Hubble—View a gallery of celestial images and more. http://hubblesite.org/

NASA History—NASA's history office includes original documents, sound clips, and footage. http://history.nasa.gov/

PBS Space Stations—View new frontiers in space. http://www.pbs.org/spacestation/

International Space Station—Take a virtual visit. http://spaceflight.nasa.gov/station/flash/modules.html

SOHO—The latest information on solar research. http://umbra.nascom.nasa.gov/images/latest.html

Space.com—Up-to-the-minute news about space exploration. www.space.com

Apollo-Soyuz Test Project—Read an overview. http://science.ksc.nasa.gov/history/astp/astp.html

ABOUT THE AUTHOR
Robin Kerrod's best-selling titles such as *Hubble, Apollo, Voyager,* and *Illustrated History of NASA,* chronicles our exciting explorations of the space frontier. Kerrod is a former winner of Britain's prestigious COPUS science book prize.